CRUISING ON QUEEN ELIZABETH

And other adventures

For friends old and new

CHAPTER 1

Distance travelled: 356 miles 572 Kilometres

Woke up bright and early at 6am. Let me rephrase that, woke up, slitty-eyed from lack of sleep, in the pitch dark at the ungodly hour of 6am. Got dressed, threw toiletries in the cases and cases into the car. Spencer, our neighbour, was late. Ross had to go next door and wake him. I really must start lying to him about set off times.

Our queen awaits.

Arrived at the airport at 9am. It was bitterly cold -9°C. Special Assistance was short staffed. I know it was New Year's Day but you have to book well in advance, so they know how many passengers they'll be getting and the flight times. We had to book in ourselves to save time and all the staff were friendly and helpful. I love it when you can chat and banter with the staff, rather than the stern, officious types. I was allowed to drive the scooter to the plane door myself.

The wheelchair pusher arrived. It seems Edinburgh airport only employ real characters for this job so he kept us amused as he whisked Ross through, what felt like, 50 miles of corridors. He was obviously rushed but never showed impatience or irritation. The bus was far more comfortable than last time and I was able to drive the scooter up the ramp. There was one other disabled lady and her husband. We passed a fleet of purple Flybe planes, all small and propeller - Bombardier Dash 8 Q400, not jets. Ross was thrilled as he's never been on a small propeller plane before and I haven't been on one since 1964. I drove the scooter up the ramp to the plane door and the crew just transferred it to the adjoining ramp to the hold. No fussing about duct tape on the terminals, they were happy as long as the key was out.

Surprisingly the seats were roomier than the extortionate upgrade I paid for last time to "premium" economy on British Airways. The crew were lovely, efficient and friendly. I'm very impressed with Flybe and will definitely use them again if they survive their financial difficulties. A lovely short flight and soon we were circling around Southampton. I have never seen so many different boats before. The long, wide river, a confluence of several rivers, had a section of houseboats, further on another housed yachts, then barges, yet another with small jet boats, it was wonderful to see them but as we reached the coast, I didn't spot our ship. After the panic of cancelled flights the night before our last cruise, we decided to go down to Southampton two days early in case of inclement weather or other flight delays.

The taxi driver was waiting for us at the baggage carousel and soon had us at the Holiday Inn Express, Southampton West. The first voice we heard was South African. Melissa, the receptionist, has only been here a few months but is very homesick. We were too early for check-in but they put our cases in a locked room and told us to help ourselves to free tea or coffee and we could sit in a little lounge or the restaurant. Next a South African couple arrived, he was born in Scotland like me and she was born in Durban the same as Ross. The wife spoke to me but he kept turning his back and obviously didn't want us joining the conversation. He looked like a Rod Stewart wannabe. I guess I would be grumpy too if the effect I was going for instead turned into Oliver Reed - in his later years.

Ross went to bed and I did not so much fall asleep as passed out. I got up later and had a pizza in the hotel. It was delicious but far too big for me so I took a doggy bag to the room for Ross but he slept through until the next afternoon. I sat in the lounge, had tea and read my kindle until bedtime. My friend, Kay, from Bristol was going to come through and see us before we left but she phoned to say she had a terrible lurgy and felt like she'd swallowed broken glass. She told me her cousin had it too and it was a very nasty flu. She didn't want to infect us and spoil our holiday so wouldn't be coming. She then told me that she'd had a surprise for me… her youngest sister, Hilary from USA, was visiting and was going to come with her but had gone on to London instead. I grew up across the road from their family in SA. We had visited Kay when Anne was over from Australia and had seen Doug before the last cruise and were meeting up with him again. I cried with disappointment, I so wanted to see Hilary as she is the only one I haven't seen for about 40 years. I'll just have to save hard and go to New York and meet her there one day. John sadly passed away last year and the 4 remaining siblings each live on a different continent but they are close, I promise.

The next morning I had breakfast then got a taxi to West Quay shopping centre. I had bought 2 pretty foldable sticks last time for the flights but they have tiny, hard handles and they kept slipping from under me on the wooden floor at home. I left my winter jacket at home and forgot my gloves and it is freezing today. So, I'm looking for new sticks, a throw or large scarf, gloves and a travel pillow.

The Bargate Southampton.

The only scarf I could find that I liked was a snip on sale at £119... really? I don't know whether it's because I haven't been shopping for years but everyone seems insane. Poor little children are being dragged from shop to shop, tired and bored, their mothers yelling at them while frantically searching for a bargain. Clothes littered the floor as they knocked them off the rails. I'm tired and bored too but no-one is shouting at me...yet.

I discovered Argos wasn't even in the centre so found myself at the Bargate. It was built in the 1100's and mostly used as a prison and for council meetings and/or courts. Very handy as a court as when convicted you were moved to the room next door which was your cell.

Argos appeared in the distance but they only had one each of different sticks. Made my way dubiously, as advised, to Kath Kidson. A small, crowded shop which instantly tattooed bright colours and flowers on my inner eye lids, it looked like the aftermath of an explosion in a flower shop. Now I love colour and I like flowers but there is a limit my senses can stand all in one go. I saw a tiny bag for £45 and no sticks but probably wouldn't be able to afford them and would need to wear sunglasses to use them in the dark.

Decided I was being daft as I really needed new sticks but they're pretty useless if you don't feel safe using them. What law says they have to match? It was fashionable to wear odd socks and mismatched earrings a while ago so I'll just start my own trend. Back out into the biting cold to

Argos and got one blue and one red. The gel handles are great and they are much sturdier and make me feel secure. The lady who served me then sent me off to Primark, by now frostbite was a distinct possibility and I was exhausted. I thought I'd already been there but it must be the only shop I missed in Southampton.

Found a lovely large, warm scarf/throw, lined gloves and a cat-motif embroidered travel cushion, all very cheap. I got the cashier to separate the gloves for me so I could put them on my frozen fingers straightaway. Outside I went to a bin which was surrounded by benches and took off the label for the scarf and put it round my shoulders. "That looks lovely and warm", a voice behind me said. "It is, I was frozen stupid," I replied then turned around to see two homeless men on a bench. I immediately felt guilty as I was about to embark on a fabulous cruise in my lovely warm scarf and gloves.

They chatted quietly between themselves but I caught the softly spoken words " cold and hungry". I didn't like to just go up to them and offer them money as they hadn't been begging. I had an idea. I had been looking for a charity shop to offload my old sticks as I now had 4 walking sticks crammed between my knees and was knackered so I asked the men if they could do me a favour, did they know someone who could use the sticks. The spokesman of the two said "the old man". So I gave them the sticks and a tenner and told them to get some food but I wouldn't blame them if they bought more alcohol to blot out the bitter cold and their misery. There were many homeless people in Southampton.

After returning to the centre I had a cup of tea and a slice of cake then drove about, trying to find my way out, until I got directions to a street from a lovely couple. The road was very busy and there was no stopping area for a taxi to pull over. My battery then died. From previous experience I learned if I switched the scooter off and waited a minute it would then take me a few yards further. I limped it to a car park where a taxi could pull over and rang one. The woman said it would be half an hour. I explained my battery was dead, I couldn't go to shelter from the wind and was frozen. The same man who had dropped me off picked me up within 10 minutes. Thank you!

I stop/started the scooter back to our room and was surprised that the scooter was good to go after only an hour's charge. We just ate at the hotel and the food was great. Although shattered I didn't get a good sleep.

Had a lovely breakfast then sat in the lounge area. A man came to check out with 2 supermarket plastic bags stuffed with his belongings. His daughter was in hospital and had been in a critical condition so his wife stayed at the hospital and he had booked into the hotel. I don't know whether it was illness or accident but they'd just jumped in the car with the clothes they were wearing. He said she was now complaining so, as she was a teenager, this meant she was well on the mend. He was apologetic about his lack of luggage and so grateful for the help he'd received from the hotel. You see all sorts when you travel and it was lovely to hear he had a happy ending. He was beaming from ear to ear.

Our embarkation time for the ship was 2:30pm. I had ordered a taxi for 1:45pm allowing for travel time and complications. We had just decided to get our luggage, once again in the locked room at reception when the driver arrived before 1:30pm. Our instructions had said not to arrive earlier or later than the time given. It took about 10 minutes to get to the cruise berth so we were almost an hour early. There were about 3-4 long drop-off lanes in front of the ship, separated by small pavements which held hundreds of suitcases. Staff were transferring them all to outside the terminal. Our driver whisked our cases out and helped with the scooter and we were on our way. I saw Rod Stewart/Ollie Reed and smiled but he blanked me as I expected. There are always one or two unfriendly types and he didn't look like someone I'd want to spend time with anyway, I'd be too tempted to sneak up behind him and cut his stupid looking ponytail off.

I saw two reps from Imagine Cruising but didn't get a chance to speak to them as we were ushered straight into security, no-one seemed bothered that we were so early. There was a long, snaking queue which moved quite quickly. There were huge signs informing you to empty your pockets, remove jackets or coats and belts before entering security. Everyone apart from the man in front of us did so. When we got to the door two men were directing everyone to a security check point, there were more than six of them. They nodded to me to go to the one on the left and Ross to go straight ahead. However, the young, dozy man had finally got clued in and struggled to take his jacket and belt off in front of us. We got through security quickly, registered our passports and my credit card and were given our ship cards – edged in gold this time as we have moved up from world travellers to gold. Go us!.

The grand lobby of Queen Elizabeth.

The Queen Elizabeth sat before us in all her stateliness. She looked huge, I wouldn't be able to judge the difference in size compared to Queen Mary 2 unless they were side by side. We

were quickly whisked on board, cards checked and ushered towards the lifts. The grand lobby is magnificent, I stood for a moment in awe, holding up the queue and well-organised staff.

Two young, lady violinists serenaded us as we entered. We arrived at deck 6 and I confidently led the way to room 6039 where the card wouldn't work. I kept "frying" my card on the Queen Mary but I'd carefully kept this card away from my phone and other cards and had only had it a few minutes.

Another passenger tried to help then asked me to check the number. Oh. 6093, thanks ME for making me continually transpose numbers and letters. It took me days to learn the correct number as 6039 seemed tattooed on my brain.

The QE is smaller than QM2 but just as beautiful. Surprisingly it carries only a hundred or so fewer passengers. There also seem to be more lounges etc to visit. There are only three staircases versus QM2's four. On the Elizabeth everything was centred around B staircase, as was our room, which made it much easier for Ross to get around. The shops, the Kings court buffet, the Queens room and the exit to the open deck were all centred at B. Even the theatre isn't as far a walk if you enter on deck 2.

We got settled into our room and met the lovely James, our room steward, a handsome, friendly young man. I explained our health restrictions and he said he was happy to work around us. There was a half- bottle of champagne, on ice, to welcome us on board. I went off to investigate and get our bearings. There is a great open deck on deck 10. The Elizabeth has two wind breaks on each side with some on the rails at the front, they make a huge difference, no ship hair here.

There are small tables and chairs, with footstools on the starboard side which are comfortable for me to sit in so I won't be restricted to the rear of the ship this time. Forward there are tables and chairs arranged café style. There's a swimming pool and two spa pools at either end of deck 9 with comfortable armchairs with tables under shade at the side of the swimming pools. The loungers are around the pools and you choose sun or shade. I had investigated so much I had to return to the cabin for a top up charge for the scooter.

We had to go for our muster and were dreading it. Our muster station was on deck 3. As we got out the lift Ross had a dizzy spell. The crew were trying to herd us to the right but I spotted a chair near the lift on the left. I told them he was unwell and needed to sit down.

"Don't say that," Ross hissed, "they'll think I have a stomach bug and confine me to the cabin". There was a different group meeting on the left. I know having some fluid and sugar can help the dizziness so I went over to the bar but the guy was insistent that it was closed and he wouldn't even serve a coke.

I left Ross and went to my station. We have a female captain of the ship. It was very quick, just told us what we needed to know and we practised putting on the life jackets. They scanned our ship cards to prove we had attended which meant we didn't have to go to any more for the rest

The lights of Southampton from deck 10.

of the trip. A crew member for the other group said Ross had "attended" their session so he scanned Ross' card too. He didn't feel well enough to go to the leaving do so I took him to the buffet where he could have a drink and a cake. Then I high-tailed it up to deck 10.

The pool with jacuzzis on the right, on deck 9.

The ship band, Synergy, played in the Yacht club for the leaving party. I didn't want to go to the party but was disappointed that the sound proofing is so good you can't hear the band outside the club. They are good but not as special to me as Vibz who played in The Verandah and could be heard below on the open deck on the QM2. However, as we were leaving from the home port and start of the voyage, we had fireworks across the bow as we left port. They ratcheted up my excitement, I was at the beginning of a new adventure. Most people came to watch and there was a great atmosphere. I didn't get a good picture but it was wonderful to see the fireworks shoot over the bow to the sky, being winter it was dark enough that they looked beautiful. I am so happy to be on board a ship again.

Fireworks across the bow as we leave Southampton.

I've always loved swimming and being near water, any kind, sea, lakes or rivers but never knew how happy I would be actually travelling on the sea until our first cruise. When people give me reasons why they don't like going on a cruise I understand the individual words but they don't make sense to me. How can you feel trapped when you have the vast expanse of an ocean to look at? How can you be bored when there are so many activities on board and so many new friends to make? There are new lands to discover. If you take a bus tour you can cover a lot of ground so you are not restricted to just seeing the ports we stop in.

If you are active there is the gym, you can walk the open deck which wraps around the whole ship, there are pools and jacuzzis, plenty of walking to restaurants, shops, theatre etc and you can get a lot of walking done on excursions or many people just ramble about on their own when we dock. There is dancing in the yacht club and of course, the formal dances in the Queens Room.

We don't cope well with lots of noise, people and a crowd of people moving around due to our illness. I used to love dancing but those days are long gone. You'd think being confined on a vessel with thousands of people would make us ill but there is something for everyone on a ship.

On the two Queens we've travelled on, there is rarely a huge crowd of people so you can avoid them if you like. You can choose to be fairly solitary and quiet or be amongst all the people and action.

The Lido buffet restaurant.

The buffet closes for half an hour or so between breakfast and lunch then between lunch and dinner. We never go to the buffet when it first opens for the next meal as there's usually a stampede of gannets desperate to get in first. We've never come across empty serving platters as they are constantly refilled. We go to the theatre early and wait in our seats until nearly everyone else has gone. It is easy to adapt to whatever health restrictions you have.

I joined Ross and we had a meal at the Lido. There are two stations for food, a small one and then a much larger one with the alternative Lido (where you have to pay) at the rear. The food was amazing, a huge choice and all delicious. There was always a crew member on hand to help me. They carry my plate, dish up, make my tea and direct us to a table if necessary. If you're disabled they hone in on you but in a friendly, respectful way. After dinner we went to deck 10 and were soon chatting to everyone. I clicked immediately with Claire, an Aussie who lives in London. Claire's Mum had flown to UK with her two other daughters and paid for them all to go on the cruise to Australia. Later I met the delightful Barbara, an older English woman and Irene, also English, who was on her first cruise and was travelling alone. We met a couple from Manchester and a Welsh couple but never did get their names.

When we got back to the room my bed was turned back with my nightie laid out and a chocolate each on the bedside cabinet. Ross did all his unpacking but I took a few days. Ross opened the champagne and we had it in bed. I reached to take my second sip, knocked the glass over and broke it. Oh dear, not even drunk. There was enough left for me to half a glass in my water glass. I went to the bathroom, brushed my teeth then flossed like a good girl and heard a clink. Looked in the basin to find a whole filling. It was the first molar from the incisors near the bottom front and has left a jagged edge and a lovely gap.

CHAPTER 2

Distance travelled 356 miles 572 K 489 nautical miles

In the morning I went for breakfast then down to the
Pursers Desk. One of the officers had been on the QM2
when we were and remembered me. The doctor doesn't do
dentistry, we'll be in Spain on a Saturday so no dentists and
we have excursions booked for Madeira and Namibia.
Looks like I'll have to put up with the hole until Cape
Town. One lady passenger told me she had brought an
emergency tooth filling kit with her. She didn't offer it to
me though. Ah well, I'll know the next time.

I met Lisa Harman for the first time. She sat a bit apart
from the rest of us and I wondered if she had a cold. When
I discovered she was a pianist and singer I thought maybe
she was worried we had colds! It turns out she was writing
and composing new songs into her phone. Lisa is very
pretty with twinkling eyes and engaging dimples. We were
soon chatting like old friends. I discovered her fiancé was
on the Queen Victoria and she was missing him dreadfully.
They've only been engaged since Christmas. The internet is

slow and expensive on board. Lisa is the only person who used a mobile but she kept getting cut off mid conversation with Kerry. It's bad enough getting a signal on a moving ship but when that has to connect to another moving ship going in the opposite direction on it's even more difficult.

The gorgeous, talented Lisa Harman and me, glammed-up and sparkling.

Lisa sings and plays the piano in the Commodore every evening. I marked it on my daily programme so I could go and see her.

On this first day I'm just happy to be at sea again, I tootled about the ship but mostly spent my time on deck 10. It is still fairly chilly, not as cold as Southampton though, but what a difference the wind breaks make, no gale force winds like we had to battle sometimes on QM2. Most of the doors to deck 10 are self-opening with buttons to press which makes it much easier for me. I no longer have to rely on someone wandering by to open them for me. The QE feels more disabled friendly. Ross gets up and roams around the ship himself. There's always someone to chat to and we meet up either on Deck 10 or the Lido.

One couple were both seasick so I told them I had seen the wrist bands in the souvenir shop. The husband told me sheepishly that he'd tried to make it back to the room but was 3 doors away when he realised he wouldn't make it. He grabbed a housekeeping cart and threw up on the clean towels. I said the cleaner was probably pleased as it would be much easier to wash the towels than clean the carpets and possibly walls. He said she was very kind and concerned. They disappeared and came up later with their wristbands on and said it was helping. On the first night they went to the Britannia for their meal, they greeted their neighbours, asked how they were and sat down. The following night the neighbours were gone. The waiter said they'd asked to be moved, he said he wouldn't normally tell them but they seemed like a lovely couple and he couldn't understand the request to move. Apparently to some people saying "Hello, how are you?" is too familiar.

One lady told us that her husband intensely dislikes wearing a jacket to dinner so he wore a shirt and tie and a very smart cardigan which is designed to look like a jacket. The maitre'd asked him to go and get his jacket, he refused. The maitre'd brought him a jacket but he refused to wear it. The m'd then suggested he put it on the back of his chair, when the husband still refused, his wife took it and put it on the back of her chair. It appears that as long as any chair is wearing a jacket all is well with the world. To be fair, we know when we book these cruises what the dress code is. The captains say it is at the insistence of the majority of guests. There are also more areas on QE where a man can go without a suit on formal nights but this is the reason that

Ross prefers the Lido, also that we can choose when and what we want to eat.

After dinner I went to the bottom of the starboard side on deck 10 and met Paul and a lady whose name I didn't catch. Paul is a cheeky Scouser (his words not mine), a builder and ex-forces from Liverpool (for those who don't know what a Scouser is). Paul was travelling with his father-in-law and it was his first cruise. I thought straight away that he was military from his posture. British armed forces are also usually able to talk to anyone, no matter their status, about anything.

They were having an in-depth discussion about whether we are alone in the universe. I joined in with my tuppence worth. We went from the sublime to the ridiculous but our conclusion was that the whole universe is populated with intelligent life. Every few years they pop over to see how we're doing but when they see all the wars, racial hatred, religious hatred, destruction of our planet etc. they tootle back and report that we are not civilised enough to join them yet.

We then got onto the topic of ghosts. It's amazing how many people have unexplained experiences but fear talking about them in case people think they're nut jobs. Maybe we have all experienced something and just keep quiet. I've had nothing in this house but there were definitely strange things happening in our last two houses. Paul had quite a few spooky stories to tell. He said 'people our age' and I thought – I'll take that. He later said he was 52 and I thought – yes, I'll definitely take that. We went on to discuss books and favourite authors and Trump. Fortunately, we all had the same view of the latter – very negative. He's a gift to comedians but for the rest of us with half a brain he's terrifying. It was wonderful being with intelligent people with enquiring minds who were willing to discuss anything. We fed and bounced off each other, the thoughts and ideas flying. I got to my cabin at 3 am but it was worth it. We had to put our clocks forward by an hour. There should only be two clock changes for us as SA is only 2 hours ahead.

Vigo harbour.

The next morning was our first stop, Vigo in Spain. There is a huge shopping mall right opposite where the ship docks but there is a walkway over to the old town. There weren't any suitable excursions as they all involved a lot of walking. Ross stayed on board and I set off to the mall. I found a pharmacy and with a bit of sign language managed to convey that I had a hole in my tooth but they didn't have any temporary fillings.

The top of the walkway to Vigo.

There was quite a long ramp down from the customs building to the mall and the lengthy walkway to the old town was uphill. The scooter battery goes a long way on flat ground but ramps and hills or carpets drain it faster. So, I couldn't go too far but got to the old town for my first experience of Spain. Vigo is huge but I was delighted that it was very Spanish not the usual high streets where you could be in any country in the world.

Vigo.

I enjoyed seeing the lovely old buildings and steep road. There were a few tourist shops and as soon as they saw me get off the scooter with my sticks they rushed to the door to ask what I wanted to see and they would bring it out for me. I bought a lovely scarf, a fridge magnet and some postcards then made my way back. Once I got through security there were a few duty-free shops and I bought two pretty handbags. I met up with Ross and we sat on deck people-watching and enjoying the view of Vigo. We had another delicious meal.

At 8:30 we went to the Royal Court theatre on deck 1 to see Roy Walker of "Catchphrase" fame. We sat right at the front and I left my scooter at the side of the stage. They played some lovely Irish jigs before he came out. He was really funny and had us in stitches. He said Belfast wasn't twinned with anyone, but they used to have a suicide pact with Beirut. He then sang 'Delilah' as Viagra. I will forever have those words in my head whenever I hear 'Delilah' – very funny, everyone was howling with laughter as they sang along to the chorus. At the end he sang a proper song, who knew Roy Walker had such a beautiful singing voice? The Irish jigs played again at the end. It was a very long walk for Ross to get to the theatre but it was me who got dizzy when I tried to stand up and get to the scooter. I had to wait until most people left then Ross went and fetched it to my seat for me. A South African couple came over and chatted to us, he was disabled too so understood. The man also has a mobility scooter but he couldn't get a disabled cabin so it is dismantled in his wardrobe and he is using a walker. What a pity. You have to get in fast, as soon as the cruise goes on sale as there are so few disabled cabins and sell out fast which means disabled people can't wait for bargains and sales but have to pay full price. We were very lucky getting our first cruise as cheap as we did. Ross was very tired after the long walk back so went straight to the room. I sat on deck 10 for a while.

Another sea day. I went to Deck 2 and found the theatre much easier for us both to access from there, not such a long walk for Ross. We met up and went through the Garden room which is quite beautiful, like a huge conservatory looking over the swimming pools. There was a captain's announcement that the crew were having a drill so all lifts would be switched off. Ross and I tried to make it in time but they were already switched off by the time we got to them. In stairway B there is often a massage contraption with staff from the salon offering a free sample. I have looked at this device from all angles and don't see how I can get on it as I can't lie on my stomach or back and don't think my dodgy knee would appreciate me climbing over it. The staff have never offered me a massage so I think they have their doubts too. At staircase A, where we are temporarily trapped with no lift, there are two delightful young women offering skin treatments. One is from Mauritius and the quieter one is from Namibia, the first person I've met from Nam. They are both quick to laughter. Ross has disappeared to the pool area. The girls are offering a treatment for darks rings and bags under the eyes so I am the perfect specimen for them to practice on. She dabbed various unguents under one eye. After a time she offered me a mirror so I could see the difference.

"Are you going to fix the bags under my other eye?" I asked, "I prefer matching luggage, you know." This brought forth much laughter. The collection was quite a bit out of my price range so I'll have to put up with my old suitcases once they spring back. The lifts were switched back on and we went to sit on Deck 10.

I took a copy each of my three books, 'Mikah the Meerkat Gets Lost' - a children's novel, 'Tangled Webs'- an adult novel and 'Cruising on Queen Mary 2' the story of our last cruise, and took them to the library. First, I went into the top floor which is just like an old library in a grand house with narrow aisles and spiral staircase. This was a mistake as there was a queue of people waiting for computer lessons. It was too narrow to turn the scooter round so I decided to settle down to a long wait. One woman turned around and asked if I wanted out. She made the entire line move out of the way so I could get out, I was grateful but embarrassed. I tootled off to the lift and went down one floor. It was much quieter downstairs. I asked if I could donate the books to the library and told him I had written them. He was delighted to take them.

The beautiful Garden Room.

I made my way to the yacht club to join the needlework group. I'm crocheting cotton squares to make a handbag. Two ladies were discussing books and one said she had donated the paperbacks she'd read to the library. I 'braved' up and told them I had donated 3 books -except I had written them. They asked me what they were about and when I mentioned the Queen Mary 2, one lady said her husband would be interested. She called his name, I hadn't noticed the two men sitting behind our large table, and he bought one! My first sale. And he gave me £2 more than I asked for.

We've been through the Bay of Biscay, notorious for rough seas but it was very calm. The temperature has risen since we left Europe so I went to the Pavilion Jacuzzi and it was wonderful. I decided not to battle down the staircase and instead went down to deck 9 in the lift and through the lovely Garden Room. I was able to park right next to the 4 steps up to the jacuzzi. The warmth of the water and the jets do wonders for my pain. I sat in the sun until I was mostly dry then popped my kaftan on and went back up to the deck.

Tonight is the black and white ball. I can't go to anything with a lot of people and watching the movement would make me dizzier but I do love to go down and see everyone dolled up in all their finery. There is also a Captain's Welcome Reception. It would be great to meet Captain

Inger Klein Thorauge but I'm sure it'll be packed so I'll wait for the cocktail party instead.

Apart from the guests in the Princess and Queen's Grill

A carved fruit design in the Lido.

suites everyone is allocated a seating in the Brittania restaurant. We tried it on the Queen Mary and, although the food is delicious, we prefer the buffet. There is a wide variety of equally delicious dishes to choose from and we can eat whenever we like. Ross isn't keen on dressing up in collar and tie just for dinner. I don't really care about the

A carved melon and some bottled squashes with a
pineapple fish.

dress code as I like dressing up and don't care if I'm overdressed. My kaftans get a lot of compliments and are cool, comfortable and dressy. I rarely go out at home so enjoy wearing my other nice clothes and a bit of make-up for a change.

I got a message from James that the maitre d' from the Brittania is looking for me. Oops, I never did find him. By the second day I had my own personal waiter in Reymund at the Lido and he already knew how I take my tea. Every time I go, there he is to greet and help me.

We don't have trudgers like on QM2 this time. The walkers stroll around the deck once or twice, relaxed and happy-looking apart from one. He stomps around at a good pace, never smiles and never interacts with other passengers. He has one of those silly looking ponytails, those short, blunt-cut ones that looks like a shaving brush glued on halfway up his head. Oh, for a pair of scissors in the middle of the night.

The Commodore Club is a beautiful room right at the front of the ship, you can see nothing in front of you, neither the prow nor a glimpse of a railing, just glorious sea. I think they missed a trick though and should have put a fake ship's wheel in so we could all take turns at pretending to be captain. Ross is having a rest but I want to see Lisa Harman, the pianist. I'm a bit trepidatious as I have met her and chatted often on deck 10. What if she is a miserable plodder or only plays the type of classical music to slit your wrists to? I went at 7:30pm and ordered a coca cola. A waiter came along and placed a glass container of crisps and a bowl of nuts in front of me, very nice – I thought. Seconds later another came along with a plate of tiny mini quiches and a canape on a cocktail stick. As my coke arrived another appeared with tiny samosas and pastries.

The Commodore Club.

Lisa arrived, glamorous in her black, sparkly top. I noticed she always wears black, whether casual or glamorous, but it really suits her. She is a classically trained pianist, so no plodding, and has a wonderful voice. She asked for requests and sang a lot of songs from the musicals and old classics. She held the entire audience in the palm of her hand, every man was half in love with her (one man declared his love in front of his wife) and had the knack of making every single person feel like she was a dear, personal friend. The atmosphere was happy and relaxed, pure enjoyment. Strangers at other tables nodded, smiled or made comments to each other. People swayed in their seats in time to the music. I learned you had to get in early to get a seat. I went to bed happy.

CHAPTER 3

Distance travelled: 2445 miles 3934 K 1187 nm

As soon as we were dressed we rushed up to deck 10 and there was beautiful Madeira. Oh my, what an island.

Madeira.

Most greengrocers in SA seem to come from here so I was expecting a flattish, green island. Instead it rose steeply from the sea, there are no beaches really - one has pebbles and the other black sand. Madearenses go to the nearby island, Porto Santo, for a beach holiday. Reunion and Mauritius have a skirt of lower land with fabulous white beaches but Madeira is literally a mountain rising out of the seas. Of course, being volcanic it is also very fertile so was a kaleidoscope of greens. There was a floating museum of a replica ancient ship in the docks. We had breakfast then gathered on the dock for our tour. The guide was Belgian. We had a French guide at La Reunion - fair enough as it is still part of France, a German guide in Australia and now a Belgian in Madeira. She was very good.

Only one third of the island is inhabited, the rest being too steep and mountainous. The occupied third was quite sheer enough. Because land is so scarce farmers are only allowed either one cow, one pig or 2 sheep or 4 chickens. There are flowers all year round and three crops of vegetables. Arum lilies grow wild. Every spare inch is used for cultivation. There aren't any private gardens as every scrap of land grows bananas, grapes, bananas, sugarcane and bananas. Natal, eat your heart out this is banana country. Vegetables are grown beneath the grape vines. Poinsettias are trees here, acacia and other flowers are much larger than anywhere else. Flowers grow on the edges everywhere and lawns don't exist. The ground is so fertile that flower plants are shrubs, ones we recognise as shrubs or bushes are like trees. Everything grows big. Camelias are hedges between the houses with blooms the size of dinner plates.

A valley on Madeira.

It is both tropical and subtropical. Temperature in winter is 17°C and highest in summer is about 26°C. These temperatures would suit us perfectly. I would love to live here but would never be able to leave the house. No two buildings are on the same level as the mountain is so precipitous. We stopped at a viewpoint where there was a tourist shop, 300m above sea level. The pavement was far too steep for the scooter to deal with so I didn't bother getting it off the bus. Ross just sat in the shade of the bus while I went into the shop. Amongst many things Madeira is also well known for its lace and embroidery. I could have bought the shop but settled for an embroidered bag and another scarf. I really must stop buying scarves I already have loads of them. I think I get hypnotised by the pretty colours and satiny fabric. It was only a few metres from the bus to the viewpoint, which had tables and chairs where you could have a drink, but it was not far off vertical. We were both knackered and collapsed into the nearest seats when we got there and needed the rest before getting back on the coach.

The highest peak is 1862 metres above sea level. Our bus tour took us to Pico do Areeiro a mere 1818m (5965 ft) above sea level. It was rather scary as the side of the bus seemed to be on the very edge of the precipice. It was terrifying when we had to pass another vehicle as we had rock face on one side and a nearly straight drop to the valley on the other. There are lots of aromatic eucalyptus trees. There was a lovely centre at Pico do Areeiro, the adventurous could walk up to Pico Ruivo, needless to say we were not among them. Included in our trip was a visit to the centre

View of the sea, Madeira.

where we had some bites of food, Madeiran desserts, Madeira cake traditionally made from sweet chestnut flour and of course, the famous Madeira wine.

I haven't had a glass of Madeira wine since leaving South Africa nearly 30 years ago. The history of the wine is fascinating. We had passed a winery in Funchal where there were wine casks in the windows of a car salesroom - type of showroom. It didn't strike me as odd at the time but wine is usually stored in airtight casks and stored in a cool, dark environment. The first Madeira wine came about by accident. In the late fifteenth century they made a white wine as normal then loaded it onto ships bound for Portugal. However, there wasn't enough room in the hold so the casks were stored on deck in the hot sunshine and weren't quite airtight either. In those days it took much longer than two days to sail from Madeira to Portugal. By the time the ship reached its destination the sun and air did their job and the sweet Madeira dessert wine was born.

Coming back we went the other way around Funchal. We passed the beautiful valley of Curral das Freiras where Funchal's nuns reportedly hid from pirates in 1566. The

View of Funchal.

soil is very red and fertile and you can see the streams of rock lacing straight down which are the chimneys of previous lava eruptions. It is 25 000 years since the last eruption and they calculate it will be 100 000 until the next one. So not in my lifetime then.

Back in Funchal the houses were all pretty, I only saw one or two shabby houses but the rest look like a holiday resort. but it is the vegetation and 'gardens' which really fascinated me. Our next stop was Cabo Girao, the highest cliff in Europe and second highest in the world. There is a glass viewing platform. I have always been scared of heights, probably since I fell down my Grandad's stairs aged 9 months and got a black eye. Oddly, I was less scared on the glass platform than walking on the metal grid leading to it. Ross stayed on terra firma and I stood on the platform long enough to say 'help' and for him to take a photo.

We spent so much time enjoying the views that we had to rush back to the bus then travelled back down to sea level to the ship. No wonder Madeirans are so proud of their island, it is truly beautiful. I loved Madeira and would be very happy to come back. This excursion was well worth it.

We are not sleeping as well as we did on QM2 and are finding the beds rather too firm for our liking. Although it is hot and I've been in the Jacuzzi my pain levels aren't reducing much. I mentioned it to Irene and she suggested I ask for bed toppers.

"Do they have them onboard?" I asked.

"I don't know, never been on a cruise before. You can only ask," she replied.

Me bravely standing on the glass platform of the highest cliff in Europe. Help!

I toddled back to the Pursers desk and they do! The lady phoned housekeeping while I waited. I thanked her, got in the lift to our deck and there was a man standing at our

Salmon pink sunset.

door with two toppers under his arm. He brought them in and said housekeeping would be along shortly to remake the beds. When we got back from dinner it was all done and we had a lovely night's sleep. Now that is service!

CHAPTER 4

Distance travelled: 2445 miles 3934 K 1187 nm

We have eight glorious days at sea ahead of us. My joy holds no bounds. The weather is sublime and the sea like a pane of glass it is so calm.

Leaving Madeira.

We are in the Doldrums, the area where sailors of old went crazy as they were stranded for weeks on end with not a breath of wind to flutter their sails. We're not reliant on wind and have so many activities onboard I doubt anyone will go insane.

We have quite a group gathering on deck 10 now. Megan, another Aussie, is also travelling with her mother and sisters. Her mother is an absolute hoot and always has us in stitches. Claire told me she had broken the exact same tooth as me except she was eating a chewy mint at the time, I was a good girl and was flossing. We have great fun girning and trying to hide our gaps. At any time of the day or night I meet up with someone I know and always have a great natter. Paul, Irene, Claire, Lisa, Barbara, Megan and her mother, the Mancunians and the Welsh couple were always about at different times and I always enjoyed the varied conversations.

Then there is the exception. We met a woman one night - I'll call her Irish. She told Ross and me that she is very shy and finds it hard to talk to new people but she felt relaxed with us. Barely drawing breath, she then told me everything I didn't want to know about sheep. She talked for hours. Although it was a balmy night

Sunset at sea.

and we were in summer clothes she was wearing a full-length fur coat. She told us she was hiding her smart clothes and had taken off her jewellery. I don't know whether she thought she was travelling with the captain on a convict ship to Australia and was afraid the ruffians in steerage were going to mug her but she did this every night for the rest of the trip. After a few days I discovered the others had all been given the shyness spiel and were avoiding her as much as I was. She kept bragging about the huge farm they had and the special bloody sheep they bred.

One night I deliberately tried to join her monologue and it was over half an hour before she stopped talking over me and I managed to get a few words in.

Ross dressed for dinner.

Megan has got the flu and a bad chest infection. She said there was a huge queue at the medical centre and all had the flu. So they are all confined to barracks. At least it's not the dreaded Noro virus. I feel sorry she's missing her cruise but she has a long trip ahead to Australia. I'm now doubly grateful that Kay didn't infect us by visiting before the cruise.

Irene is on her own and it's her first cruise. She's getting off the ship in Australia, spending a few weeks seeing the country then flying to Hong Kong to get on another ship home. She is quite brave travelling so far alone but has joined the singles group and takes part in everything on offer. She comes out quite tiddly at night, never drunk, and is hilarious.

I went to the jewellery making class and made a beaded bracelet. It's nice to learn something new and meet different people so there are even more to nod, smile at or chat to. I popped in to see one of the other pianists and lo and behold, it was Shaving Brush. Still never smiled nor connected with his very small audience. He's not a patch on Lisa Harman. I later went to the passenger talent contest. There were only five contenders, all men, and Shaving Brush was the accompanist. He still never smiled but was competent enough although he looked a bit bored. The first two singers were very good then the third announced he was doing a Matt Munro number. I thought – if he ruins this, I shall never forgive him- but he had a lovely voice.

Not as good as Matt, of course, but a very good rendering. The last man sang sea shanties which got us all clapping

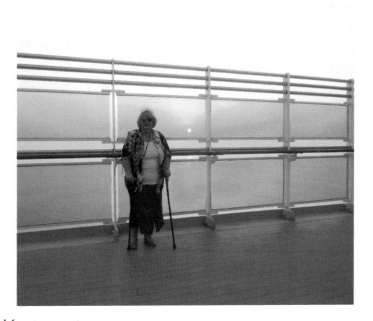

Me at sunset.

and singing along. Mouthing along in my case as I've lost my singing voice due to ME. I was never a good singer but used to love belting songs out in the car or whilst I washed dishes. I really miss it but I know three professional singers in the same situation and it must be a thousand times worse for them.

The dreaded lurgy has caught some of the crew too so a lot of the shows have been cancelled which is a pity. Ross loves Lisa too so we are spending every night at the Commodore club. She knew from our chats that Ross had trained as a sound engineer and said to him one night that she'd been playing and singing without switching the monitor on for a couple of nights. Ross was very impressed as he said most professionals can't sing if they can't hear themselves. When I repeated it to her he added "Heck, most can't string a sentence together without the monitor" and she convulsed in laughter.

She put me on the spot one night and said into the mic that I was an author, and a very good one, and then asked for a request and I went blank. I got my own back after her break by requesting that she sing one of her own songs. It was really beautiful. Jane MacDonald sings it too as Lisa gave her 50% of her rights when she was young and naïve but Lisa wrote it. She often writes and composes songs when she's out on deck 10.

A woman rushed up to me at the Lido restaurant one today.

My novel now in the library on the Queen Elizabeth.

"Are you the author?" she asked.

I didn't know how to answer and looked around as though Agatha Christie or Stephen King were standing behind me.

"I borrowed your book from the library and they told me the author was actually onboard. I've been looking out for you and recognised your kaftan from the photos. I just loved your book."

It was 'Cruising on Queen Mary 2' she had read. I thanked her then floated off, hovering about 2 foot above my scooter I was so chuffed. I'm a recognised author!

I have been grievously insulted by the budgie smuggler onboard. He is the epitome of the stereotype. Not bad looking, quite toned for his age, skin tanned to dark brown leather and has never been in love with anyone except himself. He walks the deck dressed in his tiny swim pants and a t-shirt but to the great amusement of Ross, Claire and I we spotted him stopping just out of general sight and stripping off the t-shirt as soon as he saw a woman before parading in front of us. Later on, we watched him climb the stairs above the Yacht Club and as soon as he saw women above off came the t-shirt. One time I happened to be the only woman on the starboard side and he didn't take his shirt off! I don't know if he is fattist or disablist but he had taken his shirt off for older women than me. Plus, he could give me a few years. I think all women on the ship would have been very relieved if he'd just tied the shirt around his revolting budgie smugglers though.

Today I nearly got killed by a duck-billed platypus. On most decks the lifts open out onto a little foyer but one opens directly onto the staircase. I reversed out of the lift with my back towards the down stairs and didn't stop. I felt like I was careering at great speed towards them and was probably doing full speed of 5 mph. Two couples in evening dress yelled and all came running towards me, the women in floor-length gowns. My life didn't rush before my eyes instead I could just picture myself rolling down the stairs backwards and the scooter landing on top of me. I then had a flash of memory and yanked at the keyring, stopping with just inches to spare. There is a lever below the handlebars, when you push the right side to go forward the left side moves towards you. An ordinary keyring gets jammed in the lever so I always use miniature cuddly toys as they are too fat to jam the lever but the duck billed platypus I bought in Australia had a slightly longer loop so nearly sent me barrelling to my death. My heart was still pounding when I got to the restaurant and I immediately shortened the loop. Okay, I had tea and cake first, for the shock, you know.

On my trusty steed.

Every time I get into a lift everyone flattens themselves to the walls, suck in their stomachs and stand on tiptoe. I'm getting a complex. I keep saying I'm not that big and will fit in. When you let go of the lever on a scooter the brakes kick in and you roll a few inches forward but I have it down to a fine art and know exactly when to let go. Everyone keeps raving about my driving skills especially an American couple. Most people are surprised that the scooter can reverse and are very impressed with my 2-

point turns and reversing. I had just parked at the buffet when a man came along on the only other scooter onboard.

"For goodness sake, just get off and I'll park it," his wife snapped.

He got off in a huff and sat at a table. He has one of the expensive folding scooters. When I related this tale to Ross later he said, "He can't drive it at all, he crashes into everyone and everything and his wife isn't any better. They got the scooter just before the cruise."

Now I knew why everyone made themselves as small as possible when I got into a lift with them. The next time I saw my American fans I said they only thought I was so good because he was so bad but they insisted I was a brilliant driver. I guess the two couples who witnessed my near demise by platypus would have a different opinion to the rest of the ship.

CHAPTER 5

Distance travelled: 2445 miles 3934 K 1187 nm

We were very honoured to receive an invite, as gold class travellers, to a cocktail party to meet the captain. We got into our finery and set off for deck 2. There was a queue of about 20 people in front of some closed doors to the Queens Room. I was okay sitting on the scooter but Ross was struggling a bit with the wait. Finally, the doors opened and we were off – at a snail's pace. So was the rest of the ship, apart from those on their first cruise, who were pouring in from three other entrances. It took 20 minutes for us to get in, there were crowds everywhere. I found the only two vacant seats which were apart from everyone else so we didn't even have anyone else to talk to. The rest of the people stood on the dancefloor which meant they had their backs to us so we felt quite isolated within a huge crowd. There was a free drink on offer at the door so I took a glass of wine. There was music playing and the noise from the excited crowd was getting louder. I saw Claire and her family come in. ME causes sensory overload so we are hypersensitive to noise, lights, movement of crowds etc. When this happens our brains just shut down so we are not able to think, walk or talk. I was suffering and knew that Ross was worse than me. I asked if he wanted to leave and he said yes.

The Queens Room.

However, people were still streaming through the four entrances and it took another 45 minutes for everyone to get in before there was enough room for Ross and me to get out. The relief when we got out into the quiet was enormous. We never did get to meet the captain and as she is quite short I didn't even get a good look at her. The object of the whole evening seemed to be to give gifts to the passengers with the most sea miles with Cunard which is basically the richest ones who can afford the round the world cruise and smaller cruises every year. We did get a gold pin for moving up to gold traveller. Oh well, we can say we went to the cocktail party even if we didn't enjoy it.

South Africa is just 2 hours ahead of GMT but we changed our clocks forward twice, back once then forward one hour. We must have weaved over a timeline then back again.

There is to be a ceremony to cross the equator at the pool, forward on deck 9. Those who haven't crossed the equator before are called Pollywogs and the seasoned sailors are called Shellbacks. There was a call out for all Pollywogs who wanted to take part. The pool area was packed and deck 10 soon filled up too. Ross couldn't face the crowds though so he was resting. It was a hot, sunny day and Synergy were playing near the pool. I saw a woman climbing the stairs on the port side and from behind she looked just like my Mum. I looked around and everyone was sitting happily in the sun. The band was playing a song she loved and I could just see her next to me. She wouldn't have been just sitting listening, she would have been doing a little dance in her seat moving her hands to the music. Next thing tears were running down my face, thank goodness I had sunglasses on. I saw the woman again later and even from the front she could have been a relative she looked so like Mum.

The Pollywogs had to do a parade around the pool. Next came the judge in his robes and one of those white, curly wigs, he must have been sweltering. Neptune came next with his...beautiful wife who had a flat hairy chest. Neptune used many flowery words and purple prose to describe the beauty of his wife, all preceded by a pregnant pause, which had the crowd in stitches. Mrs Neptune had a retinue of pretty girls who were actually girls and pretty. The captain and First Officer made up the rest of the panel.

The first group of Pollywogs were led to the edge of the pool. The judge read out their crimes: pressing all the buttons on the lift, spotted in the pantry stealing the bedtime chocolates, going up for thirds at the buffet etc. Everything was done in rhyme, even the captain and first officer's speeches, it was very clever and funny. The crowd were then asked for their verdict which was, of course, guilty. The pollywogs were gunged then allowed to dive into the pool to clean up. After the last of the passenger

The packed deck for the crossing the equator ceremony.

Pollywogs were done they brought out the crew Pollywogs. Their fellow crew mates really went to town with the gunging and what looked like spaghetti. I found out later it was actually cooked spaghetti. It was great fun and there was a lovely atmosphere. Once it was over they had to drain the pool, clean it and refill it. When we got back to the cabin there was a beautiful certificate for each of us with a map of the world, signed by the captain to say we were now Shellbacks.

I was quite pink from being in the sun so long so went down to the theatre that afternoon to watch Mamma Mia 2. There were two older gentlemen sitting a few seats away from me across the aisle obviously talking about Brexit.

"The awful French are going to make it as hard as possible. I've visited France, worked there and even lived there. They hate us, you know… They've never forgiven us for Bonaparte."

I was giggling at this before the film even started. I didn't know anything about the film so when I found out the mother had died that just set me off again after thinking about Mum earlier. At least I was on my own and could mop my tears without being seen. It had been a very happy day, filled with sunshine, laughter, music and moments of sad nostalgia.

If you are at all concerned about your waistline, I strongly advise that you don't make friends with the chef on your ship. Ross and I had gone for the Aztec meal for his

Our table at Alternative Lido.

birthday on QM2. We had agreed we wouldn't go to the alternative Lido this time as the meals in the Lido and Britannia are free. A delightful, softly-spoken little waiter, Jonilo, came up to my table as I was having lunch in the buffet. He gave such a lovely description of the Bamboo meal that I took a menu from him and showed it to Ross. Most people don't go to the alternative restaurant for the same reasons as us but it only costs $17.50 each. Where could you get a three- course meal for about £15 at home?

We got dressed up and arrived at the restaurant. As there are so few guests you get fantastic service from the staff.

My quiet little friend was there and he was delighted we had come. Jonilo and his friend, Alfred, treated us like

Ross and I at The Alternative Lido.

royalty. The meal was out of this world. All three courses were based on the Japanese Bento box, each was exquisitely presented and equally delicious. We had to take photos before we spoiled it by eating it.   Although it didn't seem a lot of food I was stuffed by the end. I asked the waiter to pass my compliments to the chef and next thing Karin Dicks was at our table. We both raved about

73

the food and ended up having a long natter and photos taken with Karin, she even gave me her chef's badge to

The desserts, hard to eat a geisha – she was too pretty but delicious.

keep so I gave her a signed copy of my book about our last cruise. Karin is South African, from Cape Town, and told us she would soon be making traditional SA meals on our way to Cape Town.

Karin Dicks and me.

The only problem was that Karin also worked in the buffet so every time she saw me, she came rushing out saying "You'll love this, you must try some of that." Whilst ladling it onto my plate. It was piled high every lunch and dinner when she was working. She told me she loved my book and had lent it to another passenger who had loved it too. This trip I'm asking everyone's permission to put their photos in my next book.

Although there was a sign on the QM2 which read: "They say you put on 1 lb for every day you spend on board so forget the diet and enjoy the desserts", I didn't put any weight on. I stuck to my low carb diet just eating meat and loading up on vegetables. I did have a tiny dessert after lunch and dinner and enjoyed them. This time, for some reason, I have been tempted by roast potatoes and chips. I have cold meat and salad for lunch with a roll then the gorgeous sliced fruit and fruit salad. However, when we go to the Lido at night for our last cup of tea they have these amazing rolls with either mushrooms or tomatoes baked into them. They are delicious, small and light so you have to have two, don't you? Right next to them they have freshly baked cookies of various flavours. Well, it would be rude not to. Between these and Karin loading my plates I have put on a bit of weight. It is so hard for me to lose weight being forced to be so inactive. I'll have to be extra good when I get home.

We went to the Royal Court Theatre to see John Nations, a comic juggler. We didn't have high expectations, to be honest, but he was very funny and entertaining.

I had a chat with two women, one of whom had been to SA often. We started talking about the terrible crime there. Her friend turned to her and said "Why are you taking me there?" I gave them some security advice. Common sense really.

Sitting on deck 10 one day the Manchunian couple joined us.

"Have you seen the woman with the 'arp?" he asked. We told him we hadn't.

"Poor lass. She's sitting in a lounge, all by 'erself playing the bloody 'arp. A bloody 'arp!"

The following day he informed us the poor lass was still there "playing her bloody 'arp on 'er own". However, the next day he was delighted to tell us that the harpist had moved and joined the two female violinists and was playing the 'arp with them.

"At least she's got a small audience now. We were just passing by but when they finished I gave her a good clap, to encourage her. Bloody 'arp".

CHAPTER 6

Distance travelled: 2445 miles 3934 K 1187 nm

As with the previous cruise I'm disappointed not to see any stars. One man said it was light pollution from the ship. I doubted that very much. I could understand light pollution from a town or city, yes, but the ship? There was a talk on the stars one night and most of the lights would be switched off during the talk. I had marked it on the programme then forgot all about it until Claire, Ross and I were chatting on deck 10 when we were plunged into darkness.

"Forgot to pay the electricity bill?" one wag shouted.

"Oh it's the talk on the stars, I meant to go to that", I said. Claire wanted to go too. I switched on the scooter and the tiny lights on my 'dashboard' came on.

"Great, I can see," Claire said but I couldn't, not a damn thing, not movement, nothing, all I could see was blackness. I could hear she was in front of me and was terrified I'd run her down. We were in fits of laughter as we blundered our way down the deck. There are two wind breaks on the deck but I hadn't a clue where they were either. Finally, I thought to shade the lights with my hand and I could see so both Claire and the wind breaks lived to tell the tale. The talk was on the deck below aft. We'd missed most of it and couldn't hear the rest but it was wonderful looking at the starry sky. Apologies to the man, the ship did provide enough lights to blot them out. Somehow the stars seem brighter and more numerous in the velvety blackness of the southern hemisphere skies. My Dad used to sit out on the veranda in South Africa and said he missed the stars as they weren't the same when we moved back to Scotland.

Barbara is a delightful lady and I always looked forward to our chats on deck 10. Her husband, Ian, isn't around as much. He is Scottish but speaks with an English accent as he moved there aged 11. He couldn't understand why I have a Scottish accent as I left before I was a year old. I explained that I have 2 accents, Scottish and South African and often don't know which will come out of my mouth next. I noticed that the more he spoke to me the more his Scottish accent came out. It is a second marriage for both and Barbara was stunned when her new husband spoke in a

The tanker appeared just at the right time.

her sister-in-law for a picture of Loch Lomond after a day trip there. When Ian asked why she wanted it she replied "So I know what it looks like. All I saw was shades of grey mist."

I love talking to people where one topic flows into the next and it's like that with Barbara. I told her that Ross and I had our DNA done for research into ME which led me to looking into our family tree which I found engrossing. We ended up going to a tiny village in Northern Ireland to see where our ancestors came from.

"I can't do that," Barbara said quietly.

I tried to dislodge the foot in my mouth. I had seen the Star of David around her neck. She knows of over a dozen family members murdered in the concentration camps but is afraid to look into her genealogy as it would be too heart-breaking to discover there were even more. Her daughters want to both do their family tree and visit the camps but she has asked them to wait until she has gone. She wears her Star of David to commemorate those who have gone. And so, the Holocaust affects the future generations too. Imagine having that awful gap in your family tree. Being the wonderful person she is, she then told me her favourite film is 'The Producers' by Mel Brooks as it's two fingers up to Hitler. She says that is how he should be remembered: by being ridiculed and laughed at and us living well so we can put two fingers up to him. A sad, difficult conversation ended in laughter.

Megan's mother came up on deck so we were all asking after her. She assured us Megan was getting better and would join us again soon. Her Mum is a typical down-to-earth and plain- speaking Aussie. She is very well travelled and was telling us about a trip to some nomadic Arab camps.

"The tent was very beautiful and the woman was obviously very proud of her home. She brushed the sand from the sumptuous carpet on the floor. There was ornate fabric draped on the walls but it was a tent… in the desert… in the sand."

"It was still a tent, with sand, brown, in the desert" she repeated.

She said her farewells and promised to give our best wishes to Megan. As she walked away we distantly heard: "desert".

"brown"

"tent"

"sand".

The words got quieter as she moved away. She should be on the stage, her timing was perfect and she had us all crying with laughter and wanting more. Megan was finally able to join us the day before we arrived in Namibia.

I went down to the casino but there was no-one there. Later I found Claire, her mother and sisters there. We all

Ross looking pensively at the sea.

lost our money except her Mum. There is gossip going around that the casino and pub is complaining about lack of customers. People are saying the drinks are too expensive and there don't seem to be drinks packages like on QM2. The Mancunian couple insist they drank the two bottles of wine in their cabin and they are replenished every day free of charge. We tried to tell them that even your welcome bottle of water is charged for if you break the seal. They were adamant that this was the package they got from their travel agents but we used the same one and weren't offered anything. Two bottles of wine a day would cost a fortune. Strangely we never saw them again after our credit card statements were received just before Cape Town.

I went up to deck 10 and found Ross engrossed in a conversation with Claire Layman and Irene. Ross and Claire were trying to discover hidden talents they had which would net them a job on a cruise ship. Lecturers get paid and have a free cruise but the arts and crafts people get a free cruise for themselves and a companion plus whatever they charge for the classes. Irene declared she was talentless. We were going from the sublime to the ridiculous. Claire went for her first ever art class on the ship for water colours. When I got home and looked up her website I discovered she's a very talented artist already, I loved her work. Ross does spray art which would be very difficult on a ship and resin jewellery which is doable if there was somewhere flat to leave them to harden overnight.

I said we could start a writers' group. Lots of people want to write, even if it's just their memoirs. Ross is a great writer and I have experience running a group and giving out writing exercises. I can also teach card making, crochet and cross stitch. Claire and Irene modestly said they would be our plus ones. Claire said she would specifically come on a cruise if she knew I was doing a writers group. Out of curiosity I started asking everyone I met and they all said they would love to go to a writing group onboard. Are you listening Cunard?

We saw our first sea life. I noticed lots of areas of bubbles in the sea. Then bodies started leaping out of the

Leaping tuna.

sea. At first I thought they were dolphins but they were too small then Ross said they were tuna.

They had the horizontal tailfins of fish not the vertical ones of dolphins. Leaping fish like salmon tend to leap out of the water then flop inelegantly back in but hundreds of tuna leapt into the air then dived gracefully back into the waves just like dolphins. Soon we had a crowd of people joining us at the rails to watch.

My friend, Cathy, who we will be staying with in SA told me she has booked me a pedicure as I treat. I've never inflicted my feet on anyone before so, in the same way we tidy before a cleaner comes, I booked one on the ship. I have no doubt the lady was well trained but I would guess it was fairly recent and she was new to the ship. I got onto the swivel chair and lowered my feet into the gloriously warm water. When she told me to take a foot out she kept telling me to straighten it and even though I told her it was painful she kept straightening them herself. She will need to learn that she will be dealing with disabled people and folk with arthritis and should adapt her technique to suit the client.

I was fortunate, though, that she put me in the swivel chair right next to the window. When she left me to soak between her activities, I was able to watch the sea. Two birds appeared, flying close above the waves. There was gentle, soothing music playing in the background of the salon and I could have sworn the birds could hear it. They took turns to soar in the air then swoop back down joining the other, all in time to the music. All too soon she was back, she sandblasted my feet then painted my nails with about a hundred coats. Before I knew what was happening, I had paper between my toes, paper flip flops on my feet and was being ushered out after being told it would take an hour to dry. It's very painful for me to walk without the special insoles in my shoes. Thank goodness the scooter was nearby. I went up to deck 10, which was empty for once, and sat there in my elegant footwear.

. When I tried to remove the paper from between my toes one of the flip flops fell off and a gentle gust of wind caught it. There I was, on the scooter, driving one-handed, using my walking stick as a harpoon and chasing this bloody flip flop all over the deck. Fortunately, I finally caught it and was saved from adding more pollution to our oceans.

A bouquet of carved vegetables.

There are the most amazing fruit and vegetable carvings in the Lido. Every few days more appear or others are replaced. At first glance you would think it was a floral display, they are so beautiful and colourful. You can go and learn how to do it but I can barely cook now and the demonstration is on too early in the morning for me.

We did go and watch a chef doing an ice carving aft on

Carved melon fish

deck 9. He had to work very fast as it was so warm. There was quite a crowd watching him. He produced the most amazing delicate details as his assistant handed him large tools. Flecks of ice were flying everywhere. It was stunning when he had finished.

Carved ice fish.

CHAPTER 7

Distance travelled: 7956 m 12803Km 5298 nm

Something went disastrously wrong with our alarms this morning, my phone had died and Ross' either didn't ring or we slept through it. He woke me at 10am and we were supposed to be on the pier in Walvis Bay for half past for our tour in Namibia. No time for breakfast, just threw on our clothes, very fast wash, smellies on, gathered our hats and went down to the exit. I had been very disappointed to find that all the excursions in Namibia were on 4-wheel drive vehicles and each one said for the fit and able only. They also included a lot of walking and standing around. I've never been there before and never been in a proper desert either and was desperate to see and experience it.

  Some months previously I looked up the company that Cunard uses, Red Dunes Safari, and emailed them explaining my problems. I got a reply immediately saying their staff would help me into the 4-wheel drive and I could take the scooter and there would be little walking so I booked privately with them. After struggling once to get into my neighbours Jeep, I had visions of two burly men, hands on my very ample behind, shoving me into a truck.

Ross and me at the beach in Namibia.

We were met on the dock by the beautiful Melanna. She led us to a luxury car saying that they thought I'd be more comfortable in a car. No ignominy with burly men. We have air conditioner and a chest of ice-cold beers and soft drinks. I hadn't known that Walvis Bay was British, I'd always believed the whole of Namibia used to be a German colony and was certainly occupied by them during WW2.

A warm feeling of nostalgia from my childhood in SA engulfed me as the houses were the same.

"Where are the burglar bars? The high fences? The razor wire?" I blurted out as I realised what was so different from SA today.

"It's not like that here," Melanna replied.

The houses all had lowish walls, about 3ft, and you could see into all the gardens and admire the houses. There weren't many gardens to be honest, mostly sand but with many succulent plants. We did a tour of Walvis Bay then set off for Swakopmund. We took the newly built road to the city. Knowing how long, flat, dead straight roads are not only boring but lull you into sleep whilst driving, I asked whether they had a problem with drivers falling asleep at the wheel.

Swakopmund.

"All the time," Melanna answered, "they built the road with a very steep camber so when you fall asleep your car just veers into the sand which stops it. Tow trucks make a lot of money on these roads but at least there are few accidents."

A simple solution.

Swakopmund was truly beautiful with the stunning German architecture. The police station and attached jail was one of the most attractive buildings I've seen. I loved

An impressive building in Swakopmund.

all the German street and business names. We drove
through the streets while Melanna pointed everything of
interest and added some history. She drove us to a pier
where dolphins appear regularly but they were shy today. A
man approached me with red stones on a short leather loop.
They were exquisitely carved with wild animals.

"What is your name?"

Within about 3 seconds he had my name, correctly
spelled too, carved into the stone, his tiny knife flashing

with speed. Another 3 seconds and I had one for Ross too although I had the usual African discussion as to whether it was 'Ross' or 'Rose'. He said they were very hard and would last forever. I didn't catch what they were but might even be conkers. They're as hard as rocks.

Melanna made sure to park as close as possible to wherever we were stopping and often hopped out herself to photograph buildings for me. Next, we went to the Kristall Galerie.

The police station is on the left and the low building on the right is the prison.

Unfortunately, the outside paths were too narrow for the scooter to navigate so I had to walk round. It wasn't very large though, only a few metres. Inside was the biggest quartz rock I could ever have imagined.

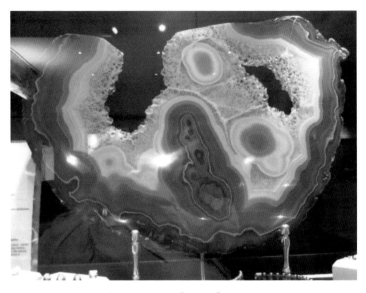

A gigantic slice of quartz.

I was delighted to find Pieterlite which is a stone only found in Namibia and looks similar to blue tiger's eye. I bought a bracelet and a few stones to add to my collection. We can carry 30kg from Joburg but still have to fly there from CT with a limit of 23Kg so I have to be careful with extra weight.

Ross giving perspective to the world's largest quartz cluster.

A traction steam train was built in Leeds, England in 1895 and shipped to the then South West Africa. It kept getting stuck in the sand every 50 m and was finally abandoned in 1897 and was left to rust. It was rescued a couple of times and renovated but kept rusting so a shed was built to protect it.

Steam train, fondly called Martin Luther.

A German Jeep was also left where it got stuck in the sand in WW2 and now features in maps of Namibia with directions such as "turn left at the Jeep". Sand really does get everywhere. We visited another tiny museum with a shop in the middle of nowhere and I was fascinated with the chandeliers made from old tin cups.

Metal Mug Chandelier.

Cutlery is used to make windchimes. Recycling really was invented in Africa, long before the word became common. Tyres make great garden pots, flipflops, or barriers to prevent damage to boats or cars. Everything is reused in unique ways.

Wind chime made of cutlery.

Our final stop was the famous Dune 7. It is 163m high and, I believe, the second highest in Africa. There were a few hardy souls scrambling part way up then sliding down, it really was two steps forward and one step back, looking like ants only inepter.

I hate hats of all descriptions (on me not anyone else) but had decided to follow advice for dressing for the desert and I was glad I did. I wore cool trousers, a long sleeved, flowing top and a hat which shaded my neck and face. It was very hot and the little bits of shade had been nabbed by early birds.

Melanna and me with Dune 7 in the background.

Soon the other Red Dunes vehicle arrived with an American couple and their guide. They had the food and we had the drinks. Although by now I was starving (my own fault) and getting dizzy from low blood sugar, I think we had the better part of the bargain as we'd sunk a few icy soft drinks already. They had more self-control and hadn't touched the food. As soon as they stopped the man rushed up the dune.

"My husband is very fit, he runs every day and goes to the gym. He's a doctor who specialises in pain control."

Bougainvillea giving a splash of colour in the desert.

I told her I could do with his services. We all watched as he ran confidently at the dune, then slowed, then slowed again then ¾ of the way up sat down for a rest as did many others. We all waved and cheered our encouragement and he did eventually make it to the top. I think both he and his wife decided he wasn't as fit as they thought he was but it's hard enough walking in sand at the beach without climbing a mountain of the stuff. Children made a better fist of the climb but were more willing to sit for a rest and thought it great fun to slide down a bit and have to clamber back up again. It was amazing how many shades of colour there was in the very fine sand of the desert. Melanna told us that the black colour on some areas was iron.

Our intrepid US doctor making it to the top.

Some women from a local tribe appeared in their traditional dress and treated us to some dancing and singing. It really made the experience special. Out in a desert, in the middle of nowhere, when the entertainment arrives, they were really good too, great harmonising.

After a delicious picnic I was desperate for the loo. Melanna went to look at the loos and came back out saying I couldn't use them. I took a look and agreed, they were disgusting. I've used all sorts of outside loos, 'long drops' and crouched behind bushes in my time in Africa but these were awful. Although the bar/restaurant had a sign saying patrons only Melanna marched in and persuaded them to let us use their facilities.

I paid my first ever bribe in Africa. I was ridiculously pleased to be held to ransom. We got back to the entrance to the harbour at 4pm and had to be onboard by 4:30pm. We had been warned the ship wouldn't wait for us and as we weren't with other passengers on an organised tour we would be left behind. The guard shouted at Melanna, she produced her papers, the same papers she had used to get in this morning and they had been perused again at the exit when we left for our tour. For some reason they were now wrong. He said we could walk to the ship which was way to far for Ross to walk. Informing him we were disabled just played into his hands. He barked at Melanna to park at the police station. As soon as she did so he appeared at the window, yelled a bit more then muttered "a hundred dollars". Melanna told him we didn't have that much money and bargained down to $20 Nam dollars (about £1). I've heard about all the bribes you have to pay in Southern Africa including traffic cops and now I got to pay a bribe myself. Obviously, it would be annoying and tedious all the time but just once was fun.

I'd never had the opportunity to go to Namibia before and I'm so glad I finally made it. It was like another world to me and I can't recommend Red Dune Safaris highly enough. My flat, summer shoes have holes punched all along them in a decorative pattern. They were filled with sand. I went to deck 10 as I thought it would be easier for the crew to clean than the carpet in my room. I had two mini dune 7's by the time I'd emptied it all out.

We have just one more sea day before reaching Cape Town then we have one more night on the ship there before

Leaving Walvis Bay.

disembarking. I'm enjoying my last sea day in the jacuzzi and chatting with friends.

CHAPTER 8

Distance travelled: 8848 m 14 238Km 6005 nm

Although we are only disembarking tomorrow we have been told that every guest and crew member has to leave the ship and go through security. We are told there will be buses which makes me think we are going back to the centre we went through at the beginning of the last cruise. I just hope their computers are working and we don't spend our entire last day at the centre. We all have to get off at the same time and no-one is allowed back on board until everyone has been processed. I can't believe they are going to leave the ship with not a soul on board.

We had breakfast then went to deck 10 until it was time to go. We met Lisa who said she and most of the crew had already been through security and it took about 2 minutes so the ship isn't being left unoccupied. We went down to the lowest deck.

There were ramps on and off the ship at Southampton, Vigo, Madeira and Walvis Bay but for some reason there are steps off the ship at Cape Town. We hadn't come across

this on the previous cruise either. The crew brought a
wheelchair

Ross with Table Mountain in the background.

contraption and helped me into it. It was like a cross
between a tank, a tractor and a wheelchair. I sat in it and the
next thing I was slowly tilted backwards until I lying on my
back! No-one could go up or down while this was
happening and the thing moved in slow motion. I felt a
proper Charlie lying there while everyone watched so
stared at the clouds and tried not to let my embarrassment

show. I was never happier than reaching the bottom and being raised to an upright position again.

The crew had brought the scooter down for me. There wasn't a bus in sight and we were directed towards a building only metres from the ship. The staff were smart, friendly and efficient, it really did take 2 minutes. When the chap Ross went to saw his birth place as Durban on his British passport he beamed and said "Welcome home". The passport control at OR Tambo airport could learn a lot from this guy.

I was able to drive the scooter up a ramp back onto the ship so I didn't have to lie back and think of clouds this time.

We spent a lovely last day on the ship. I'm not as sad as I was leaving the QM2 in Australia, perhaps because I thought that would be my first and last cruise or perhaps it's because we're spending 12 days in SA before going home so the holiday is not over yet.

Our last night was a real treat. We were to have a Scottish/South African night with mass pipe bands. As the theatre stage is fairly small it was rather wee massed bands. As we approached the theatre the corridor was lined with drum majorettes in their sparking uniforms. I meant to tell them that I was one of the first drum majorettes in SA.

The pipers outside the theatre after the show.

The MC was witty and entertaining and the pipe bands were wonderful, playing both Scottish and South African music. The wonderful majorettes were from a high school in Cape Town and we were also treated to tribal dancing and singing by the pupils. It was in tribute to Burn's Night with a South African flavour and was terrific. The majorettes, bands, dancers and singers were all very professional. It suited Ross and I perfectly as we consider both countries to be our homes. When we left the theatre the pipe bands were playing in the foyer/ casino area. We then went to the Commodore Club for our last night with Lisa Harmon. What a fantastic last night we had.

The lovely Aussie, Claire and I, trying to hide our identical gaps.

Our suitcases had been left outside our rooms the night before and were gone in the morning. We had some breakfast then went to deck 10 for the last time. All the usual suspects were there but it was only Paul and us who were leaving the ship. Barbara and Ian were there, she gave me a hug and said "said "The loveliest thing on this ship was you, you are a wonderful funny, kind, warm, intelligent woman and never ever forget that". Needless to say, I was in tears. I think it is the nicest thing anyone has ever said to me.

Irish said "You are always well-turned out and must be very intelligent because you can talk to anyone on any subject". She must have observed this because I never got a word in edge ways in my conversations with her. Claire and Irene both asked who they were going to talk to now and who would make them laugh. Lisa and I could hardly speak as we said goodbye, she's been great entertainment both in the Commodore and chatting on deck 10. Paul insisted on 2 kisses to his bristly cheek. I shall miss them all. I really loved them and they loved me back for a little while. It made me feel that even though I am disabled and unable to work I can still make people feel happy. It makes us feel part of the world as we are quite isolated when at home.

The heat doesn't cure ME but makes us feel better and helps the pain a lot. It's like having a holiday away from the illness. Perhaps the NHS should send us to warmer climes during the winter. I really need to win the lottery.

Irene and Jen.

Hundreds of people were leaving the ship at Cape Town. We were herded towards the Imagine Cruising coaches. It was a long way for Ross to walk. It was the first time there had been a bit of chaos. The reps had lists of people who were allocated to coaches according to which hotel they were staying in. Some people had grabbed the front seats although they are signposted for disabled people. Our rep soon told them to move.

The buses were parked on flat, open ground so the first step up was huge. I'm always so scared of hurting my good knee and really struggled getting up. I was out of breath and in quite a lot of pain when I flopped into the first seat with Ross joining me. One overenthusiastic rep had already gone but hadn't liaised with the others so they hadn't a clue which guests had gone with her nor whether they needed to wait for more. They kept doing head counts and ticking off names. Another couple got on and this poor lady struggled even more than me. Ross got up and gave her his seat. I was really concerned about her breathing and was seconds away from calling the rep when she finally got her breath back.

Ross sat next to a man half way down the bus. He nodded at Ross' stick and said "shouldn't you be sitting at the front?" Ross explained that he had been sitting at the front with his mother but a lady got on who needed it more than him. The man gripped Ross' right hand.

"That lady is my wife and you, sir, are a true gentleman".

Finally, we were on our way to the Table Bay hotel. Our driver had obviously noted our struggles to get on board and moved the bus forward and backward repeatedly until he was happy the last step was right over the curb so we could step off much easier. There were loads of buses arriving and leaving. There's a very long glass entrance to the hotel. It's lined with sofas and plants with doors on either side all the way down. It was packed but I managed to get a seat for Ross. I went to the lobby but was told we couldn't check in until 2 o'clock which was hours away. Bus loads of people were leaving to board cruises mingling with those of us who had just disembarked. The gigantic lobby was filled with people and had no spare seats. On returning to Ross, one look told me he was in trouble. Everyone was talking loudly, some across the passage to each other. His eyes get this pained, vacant expression and there's no point talking to him as he can't understand or reply. I returned to the lobby and found a manager. I explained our problem and he said he would get a room in the spa for us where it would be nice and quiet. He said he would send a staff member to find us and I described where Ross was sitting. I went back to Ross and waited a while.

My brain was starting to shut down too and we needed one of us to be compos mentis.

I went out the door next to us on the scooter and there were little paths with a large wall offering shade. There was a tiny garden with steps leading up to it. I went back and got Ross and parked him on the steps as there was no seat. Blissful, quiet and peace descended on us. There is nothing like the bliss that settles on you when you have silence after being in a very noisy area.

The long entrance to the Table Bay Hotel.

We discovered the wall was the original wall from the bay way back when. We sat in the sun and relaxed. After a while I went to find some drinks. There were courtesy jugs of juice inside the lobby. I could only drive with one at a time so made two trips. I never did identify what kind of fruit mix it was but it was cold and delicious. A while later the manager appeared and said his staff member couldn't find us. I apologised for moving but we couldn't wait any longer and we were perfectly happy now and enjoying the fresh air, sunshine and quiet. He sent more drinks out for us.

The foyer of the Table Bay Hotel.

Once all the people had left for their cruise it got much calmer. Everyone's luggage had been placed in a large room. When the staff saw we were disabled we were taken straight through to the next room and given our room keys straight away. Ross and I went off and found the outside restaurant for lunch. We both chose the chicken snack with a dipping sauce. We were relaxed and happy. It's a gorgeous, huge 5- star hotel. There was an intriguing, ancient door leading into the bar and restaurant. Sadly, none of the staff knew its history but it wouldn't have looked out of place in an old castle or prison. After lunch we found out our room was ready so we went up for a rest. Our luggage was in our room when we got there.

I had a nap but Ross stayed sleeping so I went off to investigate. Just outside the hotel, overlooking the bay is a double- life sized, golden statue of a cape fur seal. Many years ago, an elderly man, named Oscar, used to fish at the pier every day. One day a seal came to join him. After a few daily visits Oscar started throwing some bait then fish to the seal. The pair became a common sight. When they began building the hotel the labourers were fascinated with the friendship of the old man and the seal. Oscar was a friendly and kindly soul and enjoyed chatting to them. Sadly he passed away but his seal still came looking for him every day. The staff named him Oscar in tribute to the

Oscar with The Table Bay Hotel in the background.

old man and began feeding him too. Oscar even brought his pups to meet them. Unfortunately, Oscar the seal was killed in a boating accident and so the owners commissioned this beautiful statue in memory of both Oscars and their lovely friendship.

Ross woke up when I returned to the room. He didn't want to go down for dinner and wasn't very hungry but I needed something. I'd seen a woman get a toasted sandwich at lunch which was enormous. We decided to order room service and requested one toasted sandwich with two plates, two desserts (who could resist) and Ross wanted an Appletiser. There was a desk with two chairs which I cleared it so we could eat there. Shortly afterwards there was a knock at the door.

A tall waiter in tails appeared pushing a trolley. I've never seen anyone in tails in real life before, only in films or pictures. He looked very dignified in his tie with tails reaching his knees while delivering half a sandwich each. On top of the trolley were two plates with those large silver domes. He pushed the trolley in and stopped between a bed and the desk. He fiddled under the table cloth and voila! The trolley turned into a round table. He dug around again and came up with cutlery and napkins, more foraging produced a container of chips and a bowl of cole slaw. He took the domes off revealing one empty plate and one with the sandwich. Next came the desserts. Finally, he produced a wine glass and a bottle of Appletizer and the table was exquisitely laid. He moved the easy chair up to the table with my scooter on the other side. With a bow he wished us bon apetit and left. I just loved all the elegance for a toastie.

We divided up the sandwich, chips and salad. The dessert was divine. We relaxed and chatted for a while. Tomorrow would be a big day so we needed to conserve our energy. Later we went downstairs for a drink and to enjoy the sultry night and sea air. We got our drinks then I noticed a man standing near the Oscar statue.

"That man kind of looks like Paul" I said, although I knew Paul was staying at a different hotel.

"That man really looks like Paul" I said a few moments later.

"PAUL" Ross yelled and I jumped.

It was indeed Paul, he'd come over to visit other guests from the ship. We chatted for a while then after another 2 kisses to his bristly cheeks we said goodbye again.

We had a good night's sleep and went down for a late breakfast. My friend, Douglas, whom I had grown up with and met up with last time, was taking us on a trip around the Cape Peninsula. He called to say he would meet us outside the security gates. However, the security guard waved him in so we met him at the door. A porter watched as Ross and I dismantled the scooter in seconds and stowed it in the boot. Everyone here is fascinated by it. I guess they are too expensive here. South African prices are ridiculously cheap to us from UK but expensive to them.

We set off for our beautiful drive. The Cape is amazing in all sorts of ways, scenery, sea, beaches, mountain and wildlife. It has everything. On the previous cruise we only had one day in Cape Town so Doug came to our hotel and had dinner with us. This time we had one night on board and two nights in the hotel. It's 29 years since I've been to the Peninsula. It was so lovely seeing all my favourite places, Sea Point where Mum and I had a fabulous holiday, Bantry Bay, Camps Bay – my favourite beach, through Llandudno to Houtbay where we took the famous Chapmans Peak drive – my favourite road in the world. Next came Scarborough where I made Doug stop so I could take a photo of the place name for my cousin who lives in the original one in UK.

We stopped at Kommetjie to see the penguins. There was a tiny road jammed with cars leading to a small carpark. We waited patiently as they were only letting one car in when one came out. Doug indicated that we needed a disabled parking and the attendants who had been hanging about chatting, jumped to attention and soon found us a spot.

Penguins at Kommetjie.

When we got to the rickety, wooden, walkway we found a huge step down. I got off the scooter while Ross and Doug lifted it down. The wooden walkway was fairly narrow so I had to be careful not to go off it when on-comers were trying to pass me. We saw lots of penguins basking on the rocks in the sun. I managed to turn at the end and we made our way back to the car.

Cape Point is a nature reserve where the Atlantic and Indian oceans meet. The water at the western beaches is freezing while the east side of the peninsula enjoys the balmy waters of the Indian Ocean. The road into the reserve had huge queues so we decided to give it a miss and headed east. Simonstown has always been the home port to the South African navy and it is fairly easy to take a wrong turn and end up at a barred entrance to a firing range.

We stopped at the top for photos with the majestic views unfolding below us. I had to guide Doug to the Scratch Patch which, like many South Africans, he'd never heard of. It is set out like a miniature landscape with a tiny river and waterfall.

Doug and me overlooking Simonstown.

They bring out huge sacks (think of the old coal sacks) of semi-precious gems and pour them in the little river and all over the ground so you walk on a few inches thick of gems. You pay for an empty plastic bag (it used to be a can like a beer can), choosing a size, then you scratch in the patch and fill your bag with whatever gems you want. It's very peaceful and therapeutic sitting, scratching through the opulent colours gleaming in the sunshine. I had to be aware of our luggage allowance but Ross said he would take them in his carry-on bag if they were too heavy.

Doug really enjoyed himself and was soon digging away, choosing the gems he liked. At one stage I thought he was going to buy his own bag but I'm glad he didn't as I now have some gems in my collection chosen by him. I'm sure he'll be back someday.

Ross and I, Simonstown.

All over South Africa you find roadside markets with stalls selling fruit or curios. We stopped at the latter where I bought 2 wood carvings of a map of Africa. Then I spotted an exquisitely painted ostrich egg. The background was a gleaming black with the big 5 elephant, lion, leopard, buffalo and a rhino painted on one side and a map of Africa on the other. The problem was getting it home. I didn't have room in my case plus I'd seen the way our cases are thrown around at airports, and SA mail is very unreliable and posties chuck parcels around too.

"How much do you want it?" Ross asked.

"I really want it, I love it," I replied.

"Then take a chance," he said.

The woman called out that she knew how to pack well as lots of overseas visitors buy them and started wrapping it as she spoke. I decided to take the chance and bought it and she threw in a carved, wooden stand free. A beaded elephant keyring was added to my purchases and we went on our way.

We stopped at Kalk Bay and Doug took us to the gutting station where the fishermen clean their catch. There was one enormous seal there and a smaller one. The fishermen throw the guts to them. There were signs everywhere warning us not to go near the seals but there was a group of Chinese tourists snapping photos. Suddenly there was an

enormous cross between a growl and a bark. The huge seal
started moving towards us aggressively, we all pulled back
quickly. Another seal appeared and a fight broke out.

Doug, cleverly, started filming it. I was too entranced to even think about the camera in my hand. The second seal made a quiet exit and slid into the water while the other two went at each other. The barking was so loud and it was incredible just how big and solid they were. In a flash, the second one leapt at least six feet out of the water, grabbed the large one by the tail and pulled him into the sea. The fight was over. I think we were all equally terrified and thrilled, it was so quick and unexpected and we were all so close. Fortunately, Doug got the whole thing on video.

The moment his tail was grabbed, a still from Doug's video.

Doug took us to Kalky's, an outdoor eatery right on the harbour where all the locals go, not a tourist in sight… except us. It was packed and noisy. You made your order and paid at the counter then a woman with the loudest voice I've heard yelled your number. There were no vacant tables but when one of the waitresses saw me then made people move and got a table for us. She said her sister was disabled so she knew what it was like. I was worried about Ross but he said the food was so delicious it was worth putting up with the noise long enough to eat it. I had delicious, gigantic king prawns dripping in butter. Ross said he was going out to the car as soon as he finished his calamari but we found him on the pier. We watched the fishermen, the sea and the start of a typical South African sunset. What a wonderful day, we saw just about everything I love about the Cape in the company of my dearest friend.

When we got back to the hotel Doug parked at the door again. The same porter from the morning was there. He called four of his mates over and said "Now the magic begins". He whipped the four parts of the scooter out of the boot and put it together perfectly. His audience were suitably impressed and appreciative. He must have carefully watched Ross dismantling it in the morning and did everything in reverse. It took us a few goes to get right when I first bought it so I was impressed too. Another sad goodbye to Doug.

CHAPTER 9

Distance travelled: 9638m 15 509Km 6005nm

The next morning I had to try and post my precious ostrich egg. The Table Bay hotel is attached to a vast shopping centre in the V & A Waterfront. When the coach driver brought us to the hotel he said Victoria and Alfred and I thought he'd made a mistake. Queen Victoria's son Alfred, was sent to South Africa for his military training so it's named after him. You just go up some stairs at the spa but it was a little tricky getting there on the scooter. I had to go up one floor in the main lift then along to a lift which took me to the mezzanine. It's a disabled lift, one where you keep your finger on the button and only the floor goes up and down. A helpful staff member opened the door for me then ran down the stairs to open it at the bottom. He told me to call him when I got back.

The mall is so big that I carefully took note of shops near the hotel door and which ones were on corners of passages I needed to go down. I found the Post Office without any problems. The cashier was very helpful and I bought a sturdy box and she packed it with a bag of 'worms' for me. Surprisingly I found my way back with no wrong turns. The staff member was waiting for me and helped with the lift doors again. Ross came down and we had breakfast. Our cases had already been brought down. Every single one of the staff have been friendly and helpful. A porter took our bags out to the taxi and helped Ross load the scooter and we were off to the airport.

The taxi driver introduced himself as Charlie. He was soon chatting away to Ross like an old friend. He even talked SA politics and the daft ideas the government came up with. We talked about all sorts then he quietly apologised for not getting out of the car at the hotel. He was shot in a robbery and left paralysed from the waist down. Instead of feeling sorry for himself he got an adapted car so he could work as a taxi driver and support his family. A year or so after his tragedy the hospital phoned to say another person had the same injury so he went to visit them and counsel them. Both the police and nurses now get in touch with him when they get someone with life altering injuries. He is such a lovely, kind man I'm sure he is able to help them transition. He has no bitterness, just talks in a matter of fact way and is so proud of his family. The criminals who paralysed a decent, hard-working, black man for a few pitiful possessions can only dream of being the strong, wonderful man he is. He apologised to Ross again at the airport for not being able to help. My concern was he couldn't bring his wheelchair with him as the boot has to be clear for customers luggage, what does he do about going to the toilet or what if he breaks down? I guess he has plans in place.

We flew with SAA this time and there was no quibble at all about the scooter. Ross has a big roll of duct tape in his back pack as we had to cover the battery terminals last time but neither SAA or Flybe bothered. Gino and Dave were waiting to collect us and soon we were on our way to Benoni.

Yes, Cathy and I cried again when we saw each other. Cathy is working so we'll only see her after school and at the weekend but Dave is retired now so he was home. They cleaned the pool specially for us. The step into the pool is very steep so I sort of fell in. I can't swim anymore as after a few strokes I get so tired I nearly drown but it's wonderful just floating round on our backs. I then realised that I couldn't get back out the pool. Dave brought a wooden pallet which floated but Ross held it down for me. Dave was worried about it scratching the paint so I got out as quickly as possible. He said Cathy also struggled to get out so they were going to fit rails. The next day Cathy got me a plastic step, which kids use to reach the loo, and it worked a treat.

I didn't buy Ross a birthday present because of the weight restrictions on the plane so thought I'd buy one for him once we got to Benoni. I not only forgot to get the gift but on the actual day I forgot completely! My excuse is you don't take note of days and dates on holiday but to forget your own child's birthday! What made it worse was Cathy remembered and bought him chocolates and a cake complete with a candle.

One evening Dave said he fancied some chocolate. Ross still had some mini Toblerone left over from the ship so brought them out. Cathy, Ross and I were sitting at the round table and Dave was standing. Next thing she gave this weird cough, clutched her throat, said "nuts" and ran for her room. I was so worried and felt guilty, I hadn't realised that she was allergic to all nuts and that even the

Jenni (Cathy's sister), Cathy and I.

smell on someone's breath could set her off. I was used to
Ross' allergies but this was something else. Ross took the
rest of the chocolate to his room and I fished in the dustbin
for the discarded wrappers, tied them securely in a plastic
bag and put them in my suitcase. She came back after using
her injection and was fine. She said Dave was standing too
near her but I think it was all of us. We should never have
eaten them in front of her. She doesn't even eat plain
chocolate because it's all manufactured in a factory with

nuts. A life with no chocolate – Ross wouldn't survive. He can live without eggs and potatoes but never chocolate.

Dave, Ross and Gino in the kitchen.

We had another braai (barbecue) and Gino and Jenny came over. We were having a lovely time when Cathy's phone rang, she went and looked out the window then went outside. She came back in with my old boyfriend. He's changed a lot, dominated the conversation and, let's just say, sometimes it's better to just have your memories. He drank the beers he brought with him then left as the food was ready.

Jenny and Gino have a hardware store and I'd asked them if they could get me some gem squash seeds. Jenny brought me 12 packets and wouldn't take any money for them so I'll be able to share with my cousin, Jim and friends back home. Jim had grown some successfully in a little greenhouse in Scotland.

There was a school reunion on the Saturday but in Johannesburg, I didn't feel up to going so far and Cathy had to go to a meeting at her school in the morning so we had our own in Benoni.

Karen kindly offered to host it. Cathy managed to get in touch with Seana Trichardt and Pia, Alice and Magali came again. It was so lovely seeing them all and wonderful to see Seana, like the others she hasn't changed at all. I really did have a great bunch of friends at school and it's fantastic to fall back into them as though 4 decades haven't passed. We had a great time talking about our school days and catching up with our lives.

L-R: Magali, Seana, Karen, Cathy, Pia, Alice and me at the front.

Since I became Ill my Mum and I had a habit of explaining to new people how I was before, almost like an apology for how I am now, but we wanted them to know the real me. These old school friends treat me no different, I'm just me…Andy from school and it makes me so happy and accepted.

A terrific electrical storm broke out so everyone who had far to go dashed off. We were worried about Alice as she had the furthest to go and would be driving into it but her husband phoned to say he would meet her half way.

I took unwell going out to the car, so dizzy I could hardly move and Seana, ever the nurse, rushed to help me and Cathy brought the car to the door. It was just as well we didn't go to the Johannesburg reunuion. I hate when these episodes happen in public but after 29 years I'm used to them and I was among friends. I've collapsed all over the place, once in a fridge of cherries in a supermarket, which is why I usually use the scooter. It was a very happy day.

Pia very kindly offered to take me for the pedicure Cathy had booked for me. Pia really is a sweet kind person. Her husband, who is English, was driving so for the first time Pia was treated to both my South African and Scottish accents. Cathy's friend was much more gentle than the lady on the ship and allowed me to leave my feet in a comfortable position and she worked around that. I chose a

Ross at Cathy & Dave's pool.

deep blue polish and my tootsies sparkled. Cathy came to pick me up so my nails had some time to dry while we chatted then her friend lent me a proper pair of flipflops to go home. Mrs Olie (Cathy's Mom) lived just two doors down so we went to visit her too. It is always lovely to see her and we reminisce about the days when I used to have sleepovers at their house. We had a lovely natter then went back to Cathy's.

It was brilliant having ten days with Cathy and Dave in my hometown but with great friends there is never enough time. I wish we could live in the same town again, seeing my school friends and being able to pop into each other's houses for a cuppa and a chat.

All too soon it was time to pack and make our way back to the airport. I hid some money in the cutlery drawer for our keep and only told Cathy about it when we said goodbye at the airport so she couldn't argue about it.

CHAPTER 10

Distance travelled: 13 515 m 21 749 Km 6005 nm

This should have been the end of the story. We flew to Edinburgh and went home but fate, or the police, had other ideas for us.

When I booked the trip I was told it was a direct flight home. I assumed this meant Johannesburg to Edinburgh. Stupidly I didn't check the flights until it was too late. We were flying home with Qatar airlines which meant a short stopover in Doha. My limit for flying is 12 hours but this would make the flight home 18 hours.

The Qatar crew were friendly and helpful. Airlines seem to becoming more used to mobility scooters. Every airline allowed me to drive it to the plane door, I then showed the crew how to work the brake and they pushed it to the hold. The duct tape is still unused in Ross' backpack. I had a good natter and laugh with the lady crew member who accompanied me and Ross was chatting to the man pushing his wheelchair.

The seats are roomier and as we were at a front section we had more legroom too. All round it was much more comfortable than BA. We had an evening flight and were to arrive in Doha at 5 am, the next leg was shorter and we'd be in Edinburgh by noon when Spencer was going to collect us.

I watched a couple of films and only fell asleep at 1am and was woken at 3am for breakfast. I had an eggroll which I wasn't too keen on then some kind of very sweet and sticky cake. We arrived at Doha and the wheelchairs were ready waiting. We were taken through security, the usual bags through x-ray and body frisk, then we were left in some seats. Soon a little bus like a golf cart appeared. Due to the time difference we only had a shortish wait so no time to go for a coffee. Qatar airport is vast. It's a very long building, so long they have an elevated train running inside. We were taken past all the shops and restaurants. I saw a ladies boutique which had racks of black dresses, all neck to toe with long sleeves. They all looked the same so maybe all the racks held different sizes. I noticed that the airport staff were quite cosmopolitan and the airport

Garden at the hotel, Doha.

seemed new and very modern. We finally arrived at Gate 10 and were left in some comfortable chairs with two other disabled people.

As disabled passengers we were to board the plane first. We finally saw activity ramping up at the gate then a man came with a wheelchair for me and he told Ross he would be back for him in 5 minutes. Instead a bus driver spoke to him and he took me to the little bus. The driver said security wanted to check my bag again. I told him they had already checked my bag and that I had my son's passport and he had my cabin bag but he said that was okay. I was terrified someone would take Ross too and he wouldn't have ID on him. I was confused and upset and didn't know why I had to go through security again. I was very tired, felt very ill and had brain fog. He said it was a random check they do regularly and was nothing to worry about. They just wanted to see my bag again. It's a huge airport so it was a long way to go, past 9 gates, all the shops and restaurants yet the plane was ready for boarding. His radio kept going off and he kept replying in what I assumed was Qatari or Arabic.

We arrived at a bus charging station, not security, there was a door at the back with a policeman standing there. As I the driver helped me off the bus he said "The police want you". I was terrified especially as three more policemen came up behind me seemingly out of nowhere. All the awful tales you hear from Middle Eastern countries flew through my mind. I was herded into a small office where another policeman was on the phone. It was rather crowded with me and 4 policemen. He didn't look at me nor spoke to me. He was shouting then finally put the phone down and spoke to the others. Next thing I was taken back to the bus and driven back to Gate 10 in tears.

When we got there all other passengers had boarded except my son and the other disabled people. Ross asked me quietly what the hell had happened. It's the first time I have ever seen him angry. I shook my head. "You've been crying", he said.

"Not now," I whispered, fearful of being overheard. The crew put us in wheelchairs and literally ran outside to the bus. The bus arrived at the plane but they hadn't brought the wheelchairs. I can only stand still for 2 minutes tops. I turned around and saw the other disabled passengers on the

With model ship in Qatar hotel. Note the panda eyes from fatigue.

platform being raised to the plane without us. The movement of the platform made me dizzier. I was scared we were being left behind. A combination of lack of sleep, illness, terror and being made to stand for more than 2 minutes meant I promptly fainted. The four crew members quickly caught me and lowered me to the ground so I wasn't injured.

Ross said I was out for quite a few minutes. When I came around an ambulance had already arrived and the paramedics were doing a few tests on me. After 10 minutes or so I was able to talk again and explain my illness to them. The paramedic said my heart, BP and blood sugar were all fine and he was happy for me to fly but the female crew member said I had to go to hospital for 24 hours for observation. I started crying (like a child, I'm afraid) saying I just wanted to go home. I kept looking at the plane with longing. I turned to the crew member behind me who was one of the people who had caught me.

"You can see I'm better now, can't you?"

He agreed but the female spoke to me quietly and said unfortunately the captain had seen me faint and it was caught on camera. She said if he allowed me to fly and I took ill on the plane he would be in trouble if he had to divert the flight. I then realised all the plane doors were closed and stairs removed so it was too late. She promised that she would stay with me and Ross could go to the hospital with me but I knew hanging about a hospital would make him ill unless they gave him a bed as well.

They then took us to the airport clinic where the doctor repeated the tests, did a test on my heart and said he was happy for me to fly and gave me a letter saying so. The lovely female crew member (I wish I got her name because she was so helpful and kind) came back and said she had booked us on a flight to Edinburgh at 1am, they were sending us to a hotel where we could rest and gave us a voucher for 175 Rial each for food. They had unloaded our luggage but weren't keen on giving me my scooter for some reason. She said there were wheelchairs in the airport and hotel. I explained that meant that every time I wanted to leave the room, go for food or the toilet I would have to ask someone to push me. I insisted and they brought the scooter. I also had to message Spencer and tell him not to go to the airport but ask if could he come tomorrow instead.

A small bus arrived which didn't have a hold for luggage so Ross dismantled the scooter and the driver took it on board piece by piece. He took us to the wonderful Oryx

The cafe area with the lift going up the outside of the wall.

Rotana hotel. It was stunningly beautiful.

Ross' banana bread.

The staff couldn't be helpful enough. We had a delicious meal (using all our vouchers) and were taken to our room where we collapsed on twin queen-sized beds. I could finally tell Ross what had happened. I'd never seen my son so angry before although he remained outwardly calm and a gentleman. He said he'd wanted to punch someone, which isn't in his nature, but with me missing he didn't want to get arrested. He said everyone had been panicking when I disappeared as no-one knew where I went.

He said the female crew member was phoning everyone, the airport manager, HR and security and chewed their ears off. Maybe it was her shouting on the phone to the policeman in the office? I don't know. Ross heard her saying on the phone "No, I would never call you a liar. What I'm saying is that you're an intelligent man and you know right from wrong and this is wrong". I can't express how scared I was and I was so worried about Ross. You feel more vulnerable when you are ill and disabled and especially when you are so tired, confused and can't think clearly. I don't know why it happened, whether it was random and the policeman panicked when he saw me on 2 sticks, whether being shouted at on the phone changed his mind or whether it was mistaken identity.

My cake at the hotel – delicious.

. The ground crew themselves were great particularly the female crew member.

Lights and fountain came on as darkness fell, hotel Doha.

Relaxing in our room Ross said at least it wasn't the religious police as they are above the law. He said he saw some at the airport all dressed in black with caps on. I felt the colour drain from my face as I told him the police who took me were all dressed in black with caps.

We slept for several hours. We had another small meal which we had to pay for ourselves then went outside to a seating area which had all the comfort and flavour of the Middle East. A man near us smoked a hookah pipe – to my delight, again something I've only seen in movies. There was a menu on the table for the pipes. Arabic music played softly and I noticed that the staff bowed and scraped to the men in the white headdresses but the ones with the red and white didn't get quite so much attention. There were fountains, coloured lights and outdoor heaters although it was pleasantly warm at 20°C.

We got the bus back to the airport for 10pm. The lampposts on the roads to the airport have black Arabic writing on them backlit with colour changing lights with 2 actual lamplights at the top. It looked like rows of birthday candles lining the streets. The hotel was beautiful and gave us a glimpse of Middle Eastern culture, food and music, we also enjoyed seeing the architecture and scenery to and from the airport but I was terrified going through security again and only relaxed when I was on the plane.

I was going to say that our stay in Doha didn't make up for the trauma we went through but we really did enjoy our day there. I don't want to be like Grumpy from QM2 and let one incident spoil any of my holiday and happy memories. The people we met at the airport and the hotel showed a multiracial society and were all lovely, friendly and helpful. The little corner of Qatar that we saw was beautiful, exotic and different. We had an unexpected sojourn and enjoyed it but I never want to go back to the Middle East again. Been there, seen it, nearly got arrested.

A woman in front of me on the plane coughed all the way from Doha to Edinburgh and I came down with flu two days later. We always take First Defence before flying so I guess the little bugs managed to get through somehow and gave me an unwanted souvenir.

When we walked in the door of our house there was my parcel, with the ostrich egg intact!

Final Distance Travelled: 16 957m 27 289Km 6005 nm

For people with ME I don't want to paint too rosy a picture. At home we both spend 96% of the time in bed.

Ross sleeps for days without even eating a meal. We rarely socialise and then only in quiet places. The only people we see are carers. We both feel much better in warm weather and the cruises are perfect for us. I don't think we could cope with any other type of holiday.

However, there is always a price to pay, the dreaded Post Exertional Malaise or payback. We are both severely ill for about 6 months afterwards. Our philosophy is that we could feel just as bad anyway if we pick up a virus at home, even a cold lasts 3 months. I don't know how much longer I'm going to live, I don't know how much longer I'm going to be able to travel at all. Fibromyalgia has attacked my knees and I'm becoming fully reliant on the mobility scooter. We're going to get another scooter for Ross, there's too much walking for him even with wheelchair help at airports. I get more out of the holiday and he suffers more when we get back. Saying that he only spent 3-4 full days in bed over the four weeks whereas at home he gets up for 2-3 hours most days and a few days a week completely bedbound so it's still a huge boost for him.

For us it is worth it though. It's almost like having a holiday away from ME. My GP said "I think you are so brave, I know what it costs you when you come back. Now, when are you booking your next cruise?" We have his full support and will be saving like mad for the next one. Watch this spot….

Thank you for reading my book and please, please leave feedback on Amazon for me. Even a few words will do and don't forget to give stars, please.

My other books on Amazon:

Cruising on Queen Mary 2 and other adventures – about our trip to Australia.
Tangled Webs – a novel.
Mikah the Meerkat Gets Lost – a children's book.

10% of all royalties are donated to ME research.

Printed in Great Britain
by Amazon

36562163R00089